■SCHOLASTIC

All About Me

Art Activities

20 Easy, Step-by-Step Projects That Celebrate Kids' Individuality—and Build Classroom Community

BY CHRISTY HALE

New York • Toronto • London • Auckland • Sydney
Mexico City • New Delhi • Hong Kong • Buenos Aires

Teaching Resources

For Kate

Edited and produced by Immacula A. Rhodes
Cover design by Jason Robinson
Interior design and illustrations by Christy Hale

ISBN–13: 978-0-439-53150-4
ISBN–10: 0-439-53150-0

3 4 5 6 7 8 9 10   40   16 15 14 13 12 11

Contents

Introduction   4

What's Inside?   5

Helpful Hints   6

Connections to the Standards   6

Who's That? Chair-Back Covers   7

Through the Years Picture Mobiles   9

From Tees to Z-z-zs T-Shirt Pillows   12

Mini-Me Hand Charms   14

Flower Face Paper-Plate Masks   16

My Shadow Silhouette Portraits   20

Found-Letter Nameplates   23

My Thoughts and Dreams Personalized Collages   25

Patchwork Me Nine-Square Quilts   27

Watch Me Grow Picture Planters   30

My Favorite Things Tissue-Box Frames   34

Special People Community Tree   36

My Changing Moods Paper-Plate Faces   41

I Love My Locks! Hair Model   46

My Family Finger Puppets   48

Friends Forever! Keepsake Book   51

Stepping Out Stationery   54

Personalized Pal Stand-Up Paper Models   57

I Can Do It! Moxie Magnets   60

Special Things, Special Times Memory Boxes   62

Introduction

A child's "world view" is a reflection of his or her own feelings about self. As children develop their self-esteem, awareness of body and what it can do, and ways to relate to the classroom community and the world around them, they begin to grow into strong individuals and discover that the world is an interesting and rewarding place to be. Positive early experiences help provide children with opportunities to become secure and confident in their efforts, accomplishments, and relationships. In addition, an extensive body of research shows that a child's self-concept is directly related to later achievement in school.

The projects in *All About Me Art Activities* are designed to help build children's self-esteem as they learn about and express understanding of themselves, their relationships, the communities to which they belong, and the world in which they live. According to psychologist Reynold Bean, in *Self-Esteem: The Key to Your Child's Well-Being* (co-authored by Harris Clemes), there are four conditions of self-esteem, as described here:

Connectiveness—to develop a sense of connectiveness, children need to feel that:
• they belong to a heritage
• they are special to someone
• something special belongs to them
• their family and friends are esteemed by others
• they are important to others
• they are connected to their own bodies
• they are related to others and part of a group
• they are part of something of value

Uniqueness—to develop a sense of uniqueness, children need to:
• know there is something special about themselves
• know and do things no one else can do
• know others think they are special
• express themselves in their own way
• use their imagination and expand their creativity
• respect themselves
• enjoy being different

Power—to develop a sense of power, children need to feel that they:
• can do what they set out to do
• have resources needed to carry out their purposes
• can make or be involved in making decisions about things that concern them
• are at ease fulfilling responsibilities
• are able to solve problems
• are in control of themselves when dealing with pressure and stress
• can use the skills they've learned
• can cope with failure

Models—to develop a sense of models, children need to:
• encounter people who are good behavior models
• feel able to distinguish right from wrong
• have values and beliefs that can guide their behavior
• have varied experiences so new experiences aren't intimidating
• set goals and have a sense of working toward them
• have perspective on what is going on in their lives
• understand the standards by which their performance is evaluated
• feel they can learn and know how to approach learning
• feel a sense of order

The activities in this book allow children to explore and share their individual knowledge and abilities, develop self-awareness and self-respect, examine their relationships at home and within other communities, and learn about their uniqueness and differences. While inspiring personal expression, imagination, and creativity, the projects also help foster mutual respect and appreciation for the diversity of families, backgrounds, and situations that others bring into the shared classroom environment. In addition, the activities encourage decision-making, learning new skills, and problem-solving. And the project-related book suggestions provide a rich resource of information and models for children to explore through shared reading.

What's Inside?

Each lesson in *All About Me Art Activities* includes all you need to know to make the project—from preparation to finished product. Here's an overview of what you'll find in each unit:

Materials: A complete, easy-to-read list of the materials that are needed to make the projects is provided in this section. Most of the items are readily available, inexpensive, and easy to prepare and use.

Before You Start: This section highlights the preparations required to get materials and work areas ready and organized for the project. Also included here are suggestions about sending notes to parents for any needed materials (such as photographs) or donation requests, or to schedule volunteers for projects in which children might require additional adult supervision or assistance.

Introducing the Project: Suggestions for discussions and activities to introduce the project to children are included in this section.

Making the Project: Here is where you'll find step-by-step directions with clear, supportive illustrations to guide you through the process of creating and assembling the projects. (In addition, color photographs that show how the completed projects might look are located in the middle of this book.)

Using the Project: The ideas or activities provided in this section offer a way in which you can use the projects with individuals or the whole class.

Tips: These helpful management suggestions offer ways for simplifying materials or a process, or for breaking down a project into parts that can be completed by children working in small groups over one or two days or sessions.

Templates: Reproducible patterns that children can use accompany some of the projects.

Book Links: Use this list of titles to inspire, guide, and extend children's learning opportunities.

Helpful Hints

- If possible, try out the projects before doing them with children. This will help you to identify the necessary materials and tools; familiarize yourself with the steps; designate work, drying, and storage areas; and assess the amount of time you'll need, including time for preparation, setup, and cleanup. Gather and prepare materials for each project ahead of time. Assign helpers to distribute and collect materials.

- If you plan to use volunteers to help children complete a project, make arrangements with the volunteers ahead of time. On the day before you plan to do the project, call or send a note to remind them when you'll need their assistance.

- Paper plates, paper bowls, or styrofoam food trays make handy containers for paint. Use recyclable, plastic food containers—such as yogurt containers—to hold water for rinsing paintbrushes. (Remind children always to rinse paintbrushes before using a new color of paint.)

- To avoid waste when blending colors, encourage children to first mix small dabs of paint until they have achieved the desired result. Then they can mix a larger amount.

- Cover the work areas with newspaper to minimize cleanup. Old shower curtains or plastic tablecloths also work well and can be easily wiped clean after use.

- To keep children's clothing clean, use aprons, smocks, old shirts, or trash bags with holes cut for heads and arms. (Always supervise children's use of plastic bags.)

- Provide wet paper towels or pre-moistened wipes for easy cleaning of messy hands.

- The projects in this book can be made with materials that are easy to find in the classroom or at home. Consider preparing a send-home letter

asking families and caregivers to help you gather materials for projects by saving items at home and bringing them to the classroom. Items might include:
  – used manila folders
  – pieces of cardboard
  – plain index cards
  – magazines and newspapers
  – string and yarn
  – buttons
  – ribbons
  – fabric scraps (prints and solids)
  – old, clean T-shirts
  – polyester or cotton batting
  – cotton balls

Connections to the Standards

Mid-continent Research for Education and Learning (McREL), a nationally recognized, nonprofit organization, has compiled and evaluated national and state standards—and proposed what teachers should provide for their PreK–1 students to grow proficient in language arts and life skills, among other curriculum areas. The activities in this book support the following standards:

Language Arts
- Describes feelings, thoughts, experiences, and observations
- Uses descriptive language (e.g., color, shape, and size words)
- Asks questions to obtain information
- Answers simple questions
- Listens for a variety of purposes
- Understands messages in conversations
- Follows one- and two-step directions

Life Skills
- Knows his or her own skills and abilities, characteristics, and preferences
- Displays positive self-esteem and confidence in abilities
- Shows a desire to be independent
- Shows pride in accomplishments

Behavioral Studies
- Understands that people are alike and different in many ways
- Understands that people do some of the same things as their friends, but also do certain things their own ways
- Knows that people belong to some groups by birth and to others by joining them
- Knows unique features of different groups to which she or he belongs (e.g., family, class)
- Knows that people tend to live in families and communities
- Understands that people must learn some of the things they do
- Understands that practice helps people to improve
- Knows that people can learn from each other

Health
- Knows the names and locations of some body parts
- Understands own stages of growth
- Understands individual differences
- Knows the cycle of growth and development in humans

Art
- Knows how visual, aural, oral, and kinetic elements are used in the various art forms
- Knows how ideas (e.g., sibling rivalry, respect) and emotions (e.g., sadness, anger) are expressed in the various art forms

Source: Kendall, J. S. & Marzano, R. J. (2004). Content knowledge: A compendium of standards and benchmarks for K–12 education. Aurora, CO: Mid-continent Research for Education and Learning. Online database: http://www.mcrel.org/standards-benchmarks/

Who's That? Chair-Back Covers

Showcase these personalized chair covers at Open House or Back-to-School night.

Before You Start

1 Enlist volunteers to precut upper body patterns from two 18- by 24-inch sheets of tagboard per child (refer to the illustration on page 8). The patterns in each pair should be identical in shape and size, and the shapes made wide and tall enough to fit over the back of a student chair when the two pieces are glued together (see step 3 for Day Two, page 8).

2 Arrange for volunteers to help children assemble the projects on Day Two.

Introducing the Project

Invite children to take turns looking at themselves in the hand mirrors. Ask them to describe their eyes, hair, and skin tone. Are these features the same for all children in the class? Use children's responses as a springboard to discuss their differences and to point out how each child's own features make him or her special and unique. Afterward, tell children that they will create chair-back covers that resemble themselves sitting in a chair.

Making the Project

Day One

1 Divide the class into small groups. Cover each table with newspaper. Provide each group with tempera paint in assorted colors, paintbrushes, and containers for mixing paint. Distribute the pairs of body patterns. Then label each child's patterns with his or her name.

2 Show children how to mix paint colors in the trays to match their skin tone, and eye and hair colors. Start with a light color and add a darker color a little at a time until the desired color is achieved. Remind children to use a different brush for each color of paint.

Materials

Day One
- two 18- by 24-inch sheets of tagboard per child
- small, unbreakable hand mirrors
- tempera paint in assorted colors, including colors to mix different skin tones (such as brown, black, white, orange, red, and yellow)
- paintbrushes
- shallow containers for mixing paint

Day Two
- color markers, crayons, colored pencils, and oil pastels
- craft materials such as buttons, yarn, raffia, fake fur, and decorative paper or fabric
- scissors
- white glue

Tips
- *Do this project over two days, with children working in groups of four or fewer.*
- *Provide plastic containers of water for rinsing paintbrushes—at least one per table.*

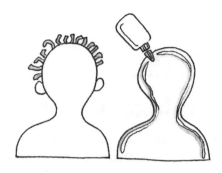

3 Have children use their specially mixed colors to paint a face and hair on one body pattern to represent themselves. Invite them to paint clothes on the torso using the colors of their choice.

4 Have them paint a back view of themselves on the other body pattern.

5 Set the patterns aside to dry.

Day Two

1 Invite children to draw details and designs on their front and back body patterns using color markers, crayons, colored pencils, and oil pastels.

2 Have children glue on craft items—such as buttons, yarn, and decorative papers and fabrics—to embellish their patterns. They might use yarn, raffia, or fake fur to add texture for their hair. Allow the glue to dry.

3 Working individually with children, help them glue the front and back patterns together along the top and side edges. Leave the bottom open to create a sleeve that can be slipped over the back of a child's chair.

Using the Project

Help children slip their completed projects over the back of their chair. Then invite them to introduce their personalized "chair sitters" to the class, explaining how they represent them. Ask children to share a few more things about themselves. Later, you can display the projects on the back of chairs during Open House or a Back-to-School event.

Book Links

The Colors of Us
by Karen Katz
(Holt, 1999)

Lena sees her skin as "plain old brown" until her mother's insights help her to see variety in the browns around her.

Just Like Me: Stories and Self-Portraits by Fourteen Artists
by Harriet Rohmer, Editor
(Children's Book Press, 1997)

A diverse group of children's book illustrators—including individuals from Hispanic, Black, Asian-American, Jewish, and Native American heritage—present themselves through both art and text.

Through the Years Picture Mobile

Introduce a unit on growth with poetry and these personalized mobiles.

Before You Start

1 Ask children to bring in pictures to represent each year of their life. You can send a note to families to request the photos (or copies of photos), explaining that the images will be cut and altered for the project.

2 Obtain a copy of *Now We Are Six* by A. A. Milne. Bookmark the poem "The End." If the book is unavailable, you might find a copy of the poem on the Internet (on sites such as www.poemhunter.com/poem/the-end-2). Or use another poem or story that talks about skills and abilities of young children at different ages or stages of their life. (See also, Book Links, page 10, for suggestions.)

Introducing the Project

Read aloud the poem "The End" from *Now We Are Six* (or another poem of your choice). Afterward, discuss the line for each age mentioned in the poem. Then invite children to tell about things they did when they were that age. For instance, have them describe what they might have done as a one-year-old baby, a two-year-old toddler, and so on. Next, help children generate a list of life skills for each age from one to six. If children are not yet five- or six-years old, ask them to name things they expect to do when they reach that age—younger children often look forward to what they can accomplish at an older age. Finally, tell children that they will make a mobile that shows things they did or will be able to do at different ages.

Making the Project
Day One

1 Divide the class into small groups. Give children the photos they brought from home.

Materials

Day One
* photographs of each child (brought from home)
* scissors
* recycled parenting and baby magazines
* 3- by 5-inch rectangles of drawing paper
* color markers, crayons, colored pencils, and oil pastels
* six 3- by 5-inch plain index cards per child
* glue sticks
* hole punch

Day Two
* three 6-inch pipe cleaners per child
* three 12-inch pipe cleaners per child
* 1 plastic coat hanger per child

Tip

Do this project over two days, with children working in groups of four or fewer.

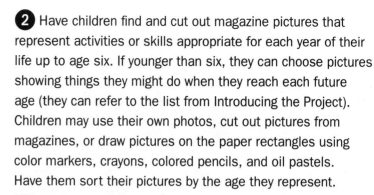

2 Have children find and cut out magazine pictures that represent activities or skills appropriate for each year of their life up to age six. If younger than six, they can choose pictures showing things they might do when they reach each future age (they can refer to the list from Introducing the Project). Children may use their own photos, cut out pictures from magazines, or draw pictures on the paper rectangles using color markers, crayons, colored pencils, and oil pastels. Have them sort their pictures by the age they represent.

3 Give each child six index cards. Have children glue their pictures for each age to an index card. Allow the glue to dry.

4 Show children how to cut a loose outline around the group of pictures on each card to create an interesting shape. Help them write a large number on the back to signify the age represented by the picture on the front.

5 Help children use a hole-punch to punch a hole at the top center of each card.

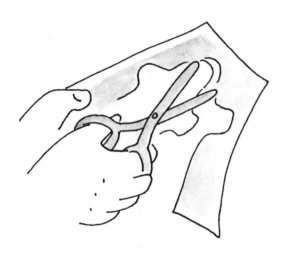

Day Two

1 Give each child a plastic hanger, and three 6- and 12-inch pipe cleaners. Show children how to thread the end of a pipe cleaner through the hole in each card and then twist the end, as shown, to secure it. They can use any length of pipe cleaner with any card.

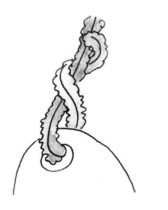

2 Have children arrange the images in chronological order and then wrap the loose end of each pipe cleaner around the bottom of the plastic hanger.

Using the Project

Invite children to share their mobiles with the class. Encourage them to tell about what the pictures on each age card represent, in chronological order, to give a brief history of their life (or to tell about what they expect to do in future years up to age six, if they are not yet six). Then create a classroom display by hanging the mobiles on a clothesline or suspending them from the ceiling.

Book Links

Pooh's Library
by A.A. Milne
(Dutton Children's Books, 1989)
A classic collection of stories and poems including the following:

Winnie-The-Pooh
The adventures of Christopher Robin and his friends, in which Pooh Bear uses a balloon to get honey, Piglet meets a Heffalump, and Eeyore has a birthday.

The House at Pooh Corner
Pooh, Christopher Robin, and their friends Piglet, Eeyore, Owl, and Tigger share more adventures in the Hundred Acre Wood.

When We Were Very Young
Verses about real and imaginary playmates.

Now We Are Six
A collection of poems reflecting the thoughts that preoccupy children as they make sense of the world.

From Tees to Z-z-zs T-Shirt Pillow

Kids use knotting skills to make a cozy pillow from their favorite, old T-shirts.

Materials

- 1 old, clean T-shirt per child
- sharp scissors for cutting fabric (for use only by adults)
- ruler
- chalk
- cotton or polyester batting

Tip

Have an adult use the sharp scissors to cut the T-shirts. Always keep sharp scissors safely out of children's reach.

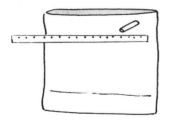

Before You Start

1 Ask children to bring in an old, clean T-shirt for this project. Send a note home to families to request the T-shirt, explaining that it will be cut and altered to make a pillow. You might suggest that they send in a favorite T-shirt that their child has outgrown.

2 Bring in a few extra T-shirts to have on hand for children who forget or are unable to bring in their own.

3 Arrange to have adult volunteers come in to help children cut and assemble their pillows.

Introducing the Project

Invite children to name some of their favorite books and tell why they enjoy these particular titles. Then ask them to tell where they like to read their books. Do they have a comfortable spot at school or home? If so, invite them to describe it. Afterward, tell children that they will make a reading pillow from one of their old T-shirts.

Making the Project

1 Working individually with children, use the sharp scissors to cut off the bottom section of the child's T-shirt just under the sleeves, cutting through the front and back layers of the shirt. When finished, the lower part of the shirt will resemble a fabric tube.

2 Lay the fabric tube flat on the table. Then help the child use the ruler and chalk to draw a line four inches from one open end of the tube. Repeat at the opposite end of the tube.

3 Fringe each end of the tube, cutting through both layers of fabric and ending each cut at the chalk line. Make the cuts approximately two inches apart. (For safety reasons, an adult should complete this step for children.)

4 Demonstrate how to knot the fringed ends along one open end of the tube. To do this, tie each fringed section on the front of the tube to the corresponding section on the back. Help the child knot all the fringed sections across that end of the tube. When finished, it will look like a fringed pocket with one open end.

5 Have the child stuff batting into the open end until the tube is full.

6 Help the child knot the fringed sections on the open end of the tube. When done, the batting should be completely encased in the tube.

Using the Project

Encourage children to show their pillow to the class and share any special memories they might have about the T-shirt that was used to create it. Children who did not bring in a T-shirt of their own can share a favorite childhood memory, too. Children can store the pillows in their classroom storage space and then take them out to use during rest or reading time. Or have children take them home for use in their private, cozy reading spaces there.

Book Links

The Napping House
by Audrey Wood
(Red Wagon Books, 2000)
This cumulative rhyming book with repetitive text and witty pictures makes a hilarious guessing game for young readers.

The Elephant's Pillow
by Diana Reynolds Roome
(Farrar Straus & Giroux, 2003)
A spoiled boy, not used to doing things for others, finds a way to solve the riddle of the imperial elephant's insomnia.

From Cotton to T-Shirt (Start to Finish)
by Robin Nelson
(Lerner Publications Company, 2003)
This book describes how cotton is grown, processed, spun into thread, woven into cloth, and cut and sewn to make a T-shirt.

Mini-Me
Hand Charms

Kids create tiny trinkets from models of their handprints. Makes a great gift!

Materials

- one 5 ½- by 8 ½-inch sheet of shrink film per child (available from amazon.com and toy and craft supply stores)
- pencils
- color markers
- scissors
- hole punch
- baking sheets
- parchment paper (for baking)
- oven
- two-foot length of yarn or key ring (one per child)

Tips

- *Work with children in groups of four or fewer to make the project.*
- *Provide close adult supervision when using an oven for the project.*

Before You Start

If shrink film or an oven is unavailable, precut 6- by 9-inch white construction paper to substitute for the shrink film (see Alternate Directions, page 15).

Introducing the Project

Ask children to examine their hands and describe what they see. Invite them to name positive ways that they can use their hands. List their suggestions on chart paper. Then choose and share a book from Book Links (page 15) with children. Have them compare the use of hands in the book to their list. Add any new suggestions to the list. When finished, tell children that they will make a miniature version of their hand as a reminder of the good things that their hands can do.

Making the Project

1 Divide the class into small groups. Give each child a sheet of shrink film. Ask children to place one hand flat on the shrink film and spread their fingers. Then have them use a pencil to trace around their hand.

2 Invite children to decorate their hand tracings with color markers.

3 Help children cut out their hand tracings. Then assist them in punching a hole about ½ inch away from the edge of the palm end of the cutout (as shown).

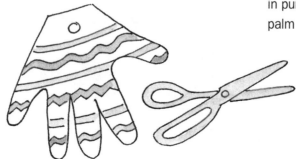

4 Preheat the oven to 300°F. Line the baking sheets with parchment paper. (Note: Do not bake the shrink film on bare metal!) Have children place their handprint on the baking sheet and then write their initials on the paper near it. Cover the handprints with additional parchment paper.

5 Bake the handprints for 2–3 minutes, removing them when they lie flat (they will curl first and then flatten). The handprints will shrink from ⅓ to ½ of their original size. Set them aside to cool.

6 Help children thread a length of yarn through the hole and tie the ends together to create a necklace. Or help them attach a key ring to their mini-hand charm.

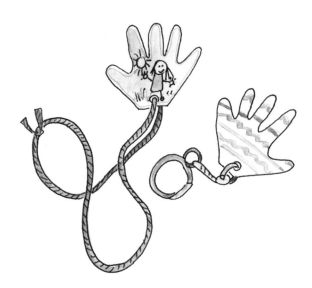

Alternate Directions

If shrink film or an oven is unavailable, have children trace their hand onto a 6- by 9-inch sheet of white construction paper. Reduce the handprint tracings by about 50% on your copy machine. Invite children to decorate and cut out their miniature outlines and then laminate them. Finally, help children punch a hole and attach yarn or a key chain to their mini-hand charm.

Using the Project

Invite children to show their hand charm to the class and share three of their favorite ways to use their hands to learn and to help others.

Book Links

Hands!
by Virginia L. Kroll
(Boyds Mills Press, 1997)
This concept book looks at the many ways we use our hands.

Hands, Hands, Hands
by Marcia K. Vaughan
(Mondo, 1995)
With the help of an imaginary creature, children discover they can use their hands to tickle, plant, feel, grab, catch, and much more.

These Hands
by Hope Lynne Price
(Hyperion Books for Children, 1999)
The simple rhyming text in this self-empowering book follows how a girl uses her hands throughout the day.

I Call My Hand Gentle
by Amanda Haan
(Viking, 2003)
This beautiful and provocative story explores themes of peace, violence, and responsibility while focusing on the many things hands can do.

Flower Face Paper-Plate Masks

Your class will transform into a colorful flower garden when children don these unique masks.

Materials

- 7-inch paper plate (one per child)
- scissors
- flower petal templates (pages 18–19)
- tagboard (one sheet per child)
- tempera paint in assorted colors
- paintbrushes
- shallow containers for mixing paint
- containers for rinsing paintbrushes
- white glue
- hole punch
- two 18-inch lengths of ribbon or yarn per child

Tips

- *Work with children in groups of four or fewer to make the project.*
- *Provide plastic containers of water for rinsing paintbrushes—at least one per table.*
- *You might arrange for volunteers to come in on the day of the project to help children assemble their masks.*

Before You Start

1 Enlist volunteers to precut tagboard flower petals and the eyeholes in the paper plates (refer to the illustration on page 17).

2 To precut the flower petals, copy the templates onto tagboard. Or trace the petals onto a few sheets of tagboard. Volunteers can stack several sheets of tagboard at a time and cut out the petals through all layers. Precut six petals per child, plus several extras to allow for mistakes, or in case some children want to use both shapes.

Introducing the Project

Share a book about flowers with children (see Book Links, page 17). Then discuss things that flowers have in common (they need soil, water, light; they grow stems, leaves, and petals), and how they might differ (the color, size, or shape of their petals and leaves, where they grow, how much sun and water they require). Wrap up the discussion by pointing out that children are like flowers—they are alike in some ways and different in others. Invite children to name some ways in which they are alike and different. Finally, tell them that they will create flower masks that represent their individuality and uniqueness.

Making the Project

1 Divide the class into small groups. Cover each table with newspaper. Then provide each group with a supply of precut tagboard flower petals, tempera paint in assorted colors, a paintbrush for each paint color, extra paintbrushes for new colors, and containers for mixing paint.

2 Give each child a paper plate with precut eyeholes. Ask children to choose six flower petals. They can choose all the same shape or mix the shapes.

3 Have children paint their paper-plate mask and each flower petal with the colors of their choice. If desired, they can mix paint colors in containers to make new colors. As they paint, children might create designs, patterns, or details that are meaningful or represent themselves in some way. Remind children to use a different brush for each color of paint. When finished, allow the paint to dry.

4 Work individually with children to help them glue their petals around the rim of their mask. After the glue dries, help them punch a hole in each side of the mask and tie a length of ribbon or yarn to each hole.

Using the Project

Invite children to put on their masks and pose for a class garden portrait. Later, display the photo and discuss how each flower and its wearer is unique.

Book Links

Planting a Rainbow
by Lois Ehlert
(Red Wagon Books, 2008)
A mother and child plant a rainbow of flowers in the family garden.

Flower Garden
by Eve Bunting
(Harcourt, 2000)
Helped by her father, a young girl prepares a flower garden as a birthday surprise for her mother.

Jack's Garden
by Henry Cole
(HarperCollins, 1997)
A cumulative story depicts what happens in Jack's garden after he plants his seeds.

Bumblebee, Bumblebee, Do You Know Me?: A Garden Guessing Game
by Anne F. Rockwell
(HarperCollins, 1999)
This garden book is filled with scents, textures, colors, shapes, and simple riddles to help young children identify flowers.

Flower Petals

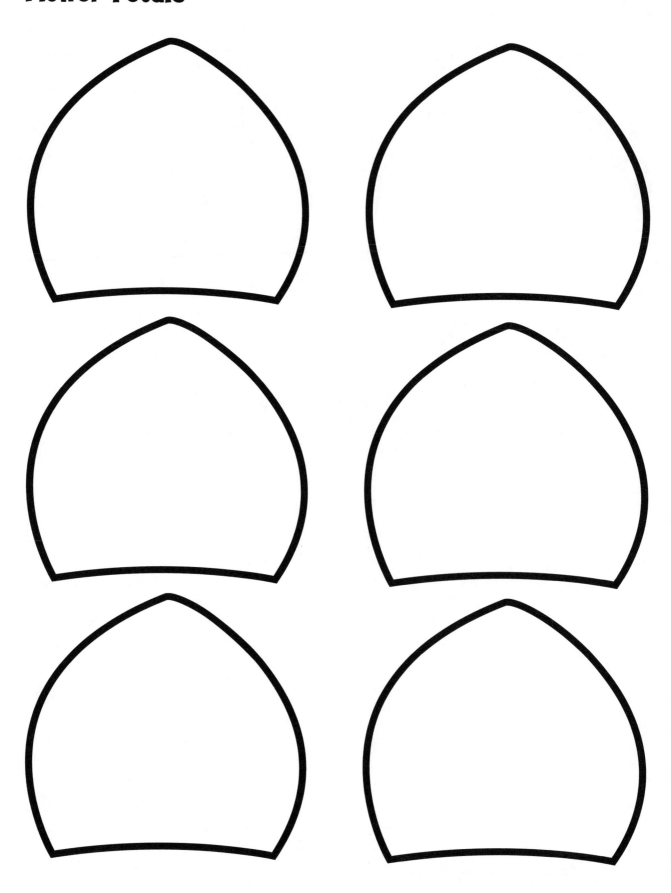

Flower Petals

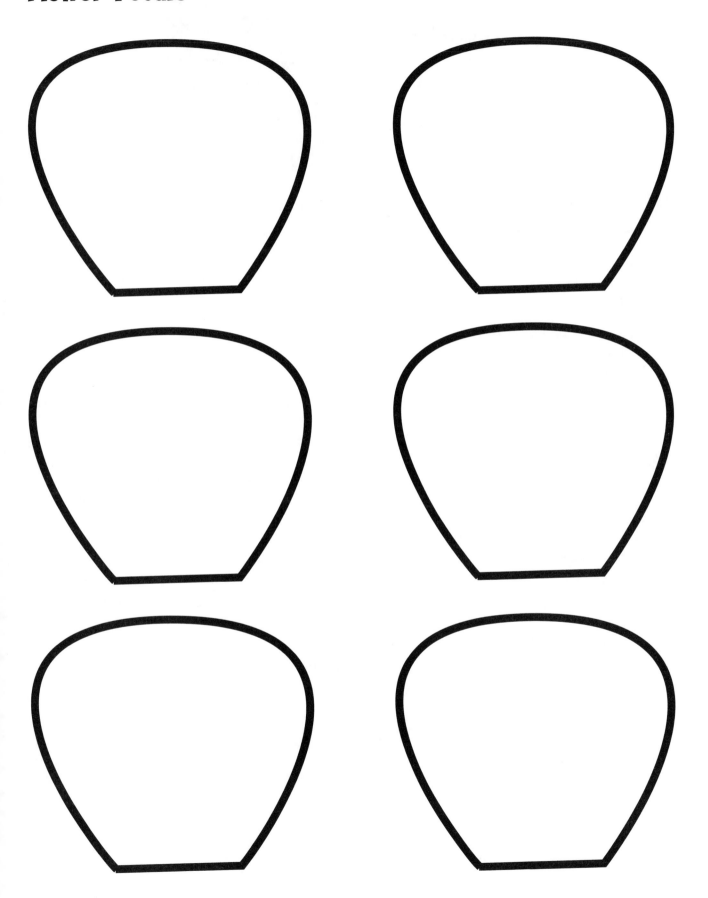

My Shadow Silhouette Portraits

Children work with partners to create old-fashioned silhouette portraits.

Materials

- lamp (a desk lamp with a swivel head or gooseneck arm works well)
- one 18- by 24-inch sheet of black bulletin board paper per child
- tape
- chalk
- one 12- by 18-inch sheet of white construction paper per child
- scissors
- glue sticks

Tips

- *Do this project over two days, with children working in pairs on Day One.*
- *You might arrange for volunteers to come in to help children draw and cut out their profiles.*

Before You Start

1 Gather a few silhouette portraits to use as models for children.

2 Prepare a space in the classroom to set up the table and lamp, checking that an outlet is nearby to plug the lamp into (see step 1, Day One).

Introducing the Project

Share a poem, story, or fun facts about shadows with children (see Book Links and More Book Links, pages 21 and 22). Then take children outside to a sunny area to explore their own shadows, or set up a lamp in the classroom so they can make and observe shadows on a bare wall. Afterward, discuss how shadows are made and how they move and change. Display a few examples of silhouette portraits, explaining that each one was created from the profile of a person. Help children define *profile*. Have them feel their own profile by running a finger from their hairline down the center of their face to the base of their neck. Finally, tell children that they will create silhouettes so they can see what their profiles look like.

Making the Project

Day One

1 Set up the lamp on a desk or table that has been placed several feet away from a bare wall. Place a child-size chair between the lamp and wall.

2 Pair up children. Have one child sit in the chair with either the left or right side of his or her body parallel to the wall. Tape an 18- by 24-inch sheet of black bulletin board paper to the wall at head-level with the child. Darken the room (close shades, turn off lights, and so on) and then turn on the lamp so that the child's profile appears on the black paper. Adjust the position of the paper, chair, or the lamp as necessary to achieve a sharp image on the center of the paper.

3 Help the child's partner trace the profile onto the paper with chalk. Trace the complete shape of the head including the facial features, neck, and back of head. Remind the seated child to remain very still.

4 Have the partners switch places to draw the other child's profile. Then write each child's name on the back of his or her profile.

Book Links

Moonbear's Shadow
by Frank Asch
(Aladdin, 2001)
Moonbear explores how light and objects make shadows. The picture sequence depicts how shadows of stationary objects change as the sun moves across the sky.

My Shadow
by Robert Louis Stevenson
(Demco Media, 1996)
Ted Rand's playful illustrations of this classic poem portray children around the world exploring their shadows.

Shadowville
by Michael Bartalos
(Penguin, 1995)
A great read-aloud with singsong rhyming verse and bold graphic illustrations that reveal the secret life of shadows.

Whose Shadow Is This?: A Look at Animal Shapes—Round, Long, and Pointy
by Claire Berge
(Picture Window Books, 2005)
This book examines different animal shadows including those of a hummingbird, gibbon, reindeer, camel, porcupine, giraffe, and ant.

Day Two

1 Help children cut out their profiles. An adult might cut out the facial features and then children can cut out the rest of their shape.

2 Have children glue their profile cutout—with the name side down—to the center of the paper. Then help them write their name on the back of the paper.

 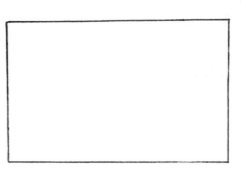 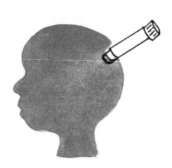

Using the Project

Display the profiles. Ask children to examine the differences in the facial features and head shapes of the profiles. Then let them have fun guessing which profile belongs to each child. As they identify each one, encourage children to tell what features they used to make their determination.

More Book Links

I Have a Friend
by Keiko Narahashi
(Margaret K. McElderry, 1987)
In this poetic text, children discover a special friend—our shadow—who keeps our dreams "secret and safe."

Light: Shadows, Mirrors, and Rainbows (Amazing Science)
by Natalie M. Rosinsky
(Picture Window Books, 2004)
This book features fun-filled explanations for simple, everyday events that happen with light.

"Shadow Races"
from **A Light in the Attic**
by Shel Silverstein
(HarperCollins, 1981)
This poem playfully describes how shadows shift with the movement of a child's position in relation to the light source.

Found-Letter Nameplates

Letter recognition is fun when kids hunt for the special combination to make their names.

Before You Start

1 Precut the 3- by 9-inch construction paper strips in assorted colors.

2 Make the project with your own name and display it as a model for children.

3 Print each child's name on a large index card to serve as a reference for the child when making the project.

Introducing the Project

Display an alphabet chart. Then write children's names on the chalkboard one at a time. Each time, ask the child with that name to point to and name each letter in his or her name and then find that letter on an alphabet chart. Afterward, show children the model of your nameplate, explaining that the letters were cut out of magazines and newspapers. Tell children that they will make their own nameplates using letter cutouts.

Making the Project

1 Divide the class into small groups. Give children the printed example of their first name to help with letter identification. Then have them search magazines and newspapers to find at least two examples of each letter in their name. Encourage them to look for large letters to cut out—they can be uppercase or lowercase.

2 Have children arrange their letter cutouts to spell out their name twice. Ask them to choose two 3- by 9-inch construction-paper strips in the color of their choice. Then have them glue a set of letters to each strip to spell their name. Invite children to embellish the name strips with additional decorations using the color markers, colored pencils, and crayons.

Tip

Work with children in groups of four or fewer to do this project.

3 Give each child a 9- by 12-inch sheet of tagboard. Help them fold the tagboard in half twice, lengthwise, and then unfold it to reveal three parallel fold lines. Have them bend all the folds in the same direction and then overlap and tape the two end sections together to make the base for a pyramid-shaped nameplate.

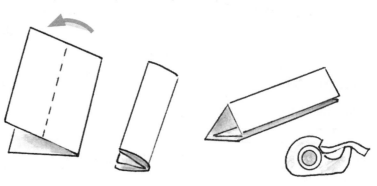

4 Have children glue one of their name strips to each side of the nameplate.

Using the Project

Discuss the letters children used to make their nameplates. Encourage them to describe and compare details they notice about the letters. Finally, invite children to display their nameplate on their desk or table during whole-class or group activities to serve as reminders of their name and its spelling.

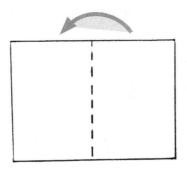

Book Links

Chrysanthemum
by Kevin Henkes
(HarperTrophy, 1996)
Chrysanthemum begins to wither when others make fun of her name. But with the help of her music teacher, Chrysanthemum's pride blossoms once again.

Tikki Tikki Tembo
by Arlene Mosel
(Henry Holt, 1988)
A folktale about how the Chinese shortened their children's names after a boy with a long, difficult name falls into a well.

Day of Ahmed's Secret
by Florence H. Parry
(HarperTrophy, 1995)
As young Ahmed completes his duties, his eagerness to share a special secret with his family grows—he can write his name in Arabic!

The First Thing My Mama Told Me
by Susan Marie Swanson
(Harcourt, 2002)
Seven-year-old Lucy is secure in her special place in the world as she remembers how her family has celebrated her name.

My Thoughts and Dreams Personalized Collages

Kids share their thoughts and dreams in these personal collage posters.

Before You Start

1 Take a close-up headshot of each child, or send a note home to families to request a photo (such as a school picture), explaining that it will be copied and returned without alteration.

2 Enlarge the image of each child as much as possible, copying it in black and white on 11- by 17-inch (tabloid size) paper.

Introducing the Project

Invite children to tell about the things they think about, hope for, and dream about. They might mention things they'd like to do or have happen that day, next week, next month, or at some time in the future (such as enjoying an ice cream after school, going to the zoo next week, celebrating a birthday next month, or being able to write in cursive in a few years). Talk about their responses and how some children share the same thoughts and dreams and others have different ones. After sharing, tell them that they will make a collage about some of the things they dream about.

Making the Project

1 Divide the class into small groups. Give children the enlarged copy of their photo.

2 Help children cut around the hair and outline of their face of their photo to isolate their head from the rest of the picture. Have them glue their head cutout to a 12- by 18-inch sheet of colored construction paper in the color of their choice.

3 Have children add color to their head cutouts with markers, colored pencils, and crayons.

Materials

- photo of each child (a headshot works best)
- scissors
- 11- by 17- inch copy paper (for photocopies)
- 12- by 18-inch construction paper in assorted colors
- glue sticks
- color markers, colored pencils, and crayons (including flesh tones)
- old magazines and catalogs

Tips

- *You might snap digital photos of children for this project. Size up the photos as large as possible and print them in black-and-white on tabloid size paper.*
- *Work with children in groups of four or fewer to do this project.*

4 Invite children to search magazines and catalogs to find pictures that represent things they wish for or dream about (such as a soccer ball, pet, ice cream cone, airplane, and so on). Have them glue the pictures around their head cutouts to create a collage.

Using the Project

Have children use their completed collages to compare their thoughts, hopes, and dreams with others in the class. Can they find a classmate who shares similar thoughts and dreams? Completely different ones? After the activity, display the posters with the title "Our Hopes and Dreams."

▐ Book Links

Allie's Basketball Dream
by Barbara E. Barber
(Lee & Low Books, 1998)
Allie becomes disheartened when she is repeatedly told that basketball is a boy's game, but she never gives up. Soon, she discovers the excitement of the game on her own.

Leonardo's Dream
by Hans de Beer
(North-South Books, 2004)
Although the other penguins laugh at his dreams of flying, Leonardo continues to practice every day. This uplifting story proves that perseverance pays off.

Little Ant, Big Thinker: Where Does the Ocean End?
by Andre Usatschow
(North-South Books, 2008)
This is a story about thinking big thoughts, searching for answers, and learning that answers depend on how you look at things.

Magical Thoughts
by Arlene Maguire
(All About Kids Publishing, 2003)
This detailed, rhythmic book includes things that delight the five senses and inspire magical thoughts and ideas.

Wish
by Roseanne Thong
(Chronicle Books, 2008)
An inspiring compilation of wishing traditions from around the world.

Patchwork Me
Nine-Square Quilts

Children can use these personalized quilts to help classmates get to know them better.

Before You Start

1 Ask children to bring in pictures of themselves, family members, pets, and so on. You can send a note to families to request the photos (or copies of photos), explaining that the images will be cut and altered for the project. Also ask families to send in old, clean articles of clothing that can be cut for use in a quilting project. Note that articles such as shirts, shorts, and pants will work well.

2 Bring in a few extra articles of clothing to have on hand for children who forget or are unable to bring in their own.

3 Enlist volunteers to precut the 4-inch construction-paper squares in assorted colors (nine per child) and the 4- and 12-inch tagboard squares.

4 Arrange to have adult volunteers come in to help children cut their fabric squares and assemble their quilts.

5 Bring in a patchwork quilt, or a picture of one, to use when introducing the activity.

Introducing the Project

Ask children to share what they know about quilts. Then show them a patchwork quilt (or a picture of one). Explain that often this kind of quilt is made to serve as a record of special events or people in a person's or family's history—each square represents something special to the quilt's owner. Follow up with a reading and discussion of *The Patchwork Quilt* by Valerie Flournoy (see Book Links, page 29). Afterward, tell children that they will make patchwork quilts to represent special times or people in their own lives.

Materials

- pictures of child, family, pets, and so on (brought in by each child)
- old, clean articles of clothing (brought in by each child)
- 4-inch construction-paper squares in assorted colors (nine per child)
- one 4-inch tagboard-square template per child
- fabric markers or chalk
- sharp scissors for cutting fabric (for use only by adults)
- old magazines and catalogs
- drawing paper
- color markers, colored pencils, and crayons
- scissors (for children to use)
- one 12-inch tagboard square per child
- white glue

Tips

- *Work with children in groups of four or fewer to make the project.*
- *Have an adult use sharp scissors to cut the fabric squares. Always keep sharp scissors safely out of children's reach.*

Making the Project

1 Divide the class into small groups. Give children the photos and articles of clothing they brought in. Provide extra clothing articles for those children who did not bring any. Also, give groups a supply of 4-inch construction-paper squares in assorted colors. Explain that children will use nine of these squares to make their quilt.

2 Give each child a 4-inch tagboard square to use as a template. Show them how to place the template on an article of clothing and trace around it with a fabric marker or chalk to outline a section of the fabric to use in their quilt. Encourage them to mark off several fabric squares in this way. Then have an adult use the sharp scissors to cut out each square through one layer of fabric.

3 Invite children to use the tagboard square and a pencil to draw outlines around the sections of their photos that they want to add to their quilt. Have them cut out the photo squares.

4 Have children cut out magazine or catalog pictures of additional things that represent them, such as their favorite foods, interests, hobbies, activities, and so on. Or invite them to draw pictures using color markers, colored pencils, and crayons on paper and then cut out their artwork. Remind children that the pictures should fit on a 4-inch square.

5 Ask children to choose nine construction-paper squares in the colors of their choice. Have them glue their fabric squares, photo squares, and picture cutouts to the construction-paper squares.

6 Give each child a 12-inch tagboard square for use as the quilt backing. Help children glue their decorative squares onto the backing, arranging them from left to right and top to bottom and covering the entire area of the backing.

Using the Project

Invite children to show their quilt to the class and use the squares to share information about themselves. Afterward, combine all the quilts to create a larger class quilt to display for class members and visitors to enjoy.

Book Links

The Patchwork Quilt
by Valerie Flournoy
(Dial, 1985)
With the help of her grandmother and mother, Tanya uses pieces of family members' old clothing to make a beautiful quilt that tells her family's story.

It's Okay to Be Different
by Todd Parr
(Megan Tingley, 2004)
Kids of every shape, size, color, family makeup, and background will recognize themselves in this simple, playful celebration of diversity.

Watch Me Grow Picture Planters

Kids make a picture record of their developmental milestones with these decorated planters.

Materials

- ruler and leaf patterns (page 33)
- one 8 ½- by 11-inch sheet of green paper per child
- tissue paper in assorted colors
- water-thinned glue (mix equal parts of white glue and water)
- paintbrushes
- one plastic flowerpot or recyclable plastic container per child
- 3- by 5-inch plain index cards
- color markers, colored pencils, and crayons
- photos of each child (brought from home)
- glue sticks
- scissors
- one wooden paint stirrer per child
- brown play dough (see recipe on page 31)
- mini clothespins (available at craft stores)

Tips

- *Do this project over two days, with children working in groups of four or fewer.*
- *You might arrange for volunteers to come in on Day One to help children decorate their planters.*

Before You Start

1 Ask children to bring in pictures that represent milestones they've achieved each year of their life—one photo per year will do. You can send a note to families to request the photos (or copies of photos) with the age of the child labeled on the back of each picture. Explain that the images will be used as part of a project at school. In the note, you might also request donations of plastic flowerpots and recyclable plastic containers, like those for ice cream, cottage cheese, or even butter tubs.

2 Copy the ruler and two leaf patterns (page 33) on green paper for each child.

3 Make one batch of brown play dough (see recipe, page 31) for every four children. You might enlist parent volunteers to mix up batches at home.

Introducing the Project

Talk with children about the different things they've learned to do over the years, such as sitting up, crawling, walking, kicking a ball, and so on. At what age did they accomplish each of these things? If desired, show a few of the pictures that children brought in and tell the age of the child in each picture. Then explain that, just as plants grow and acquire more leaves, children also grow and learn to do more and more things. Finally, tell children that they will make a plant filled with "picture" leaves to show how their abilities have grown over the years.

Making the Project

Day One

1 Divide the class into small groups. Cover each table with newspaper. Provide each group with tissue paper in assorted colors, containers of water-thinned glue, and paintbrushes.

2 Give each child a plastic container. Have children tear different colors of tissue paper into small pieces, brush glue on one side of each piece, and then stick the tissue paper to their container. Encourage them to overlap the tissue-paper pieces, covering the entire outside of the container. Set the decorated planters aside to dry.

Day Two

1 Give each child the number of index cards equal to his or her age. Then help children label each card with a number, starting with "1." Have them glue a picture of themselves doing something at that age on the other side of each card (trim pictures to fit on the card, if needed). If they don't have a picture, children can draw one on the card, or write (or dictate) a word that describes something they achieved at that age.

2 Distribute the paint stirrers and ruler and leaf patterns to children. Help them cut out the patterns. Have children glue the ruler and leaves to their paint stirrer, as shown, checking that they glue the leaves on the ruler below the "1" mark.

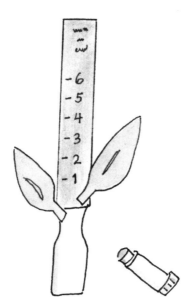

Play Dough

2 cups flour

1 cup of salt

2 cups water

4 teaspoons cream of tartar

4 tablespoons cooking oil

red and green food coloring

Mix ingredients in a large saucepan. Cook over low heat, stirring in red, blue, and yellow food coloring until the mixture turns brown. Continue to stir until the mixture thickens and pulls away from the sides. Cool before using. Store in a tightly sealed container.

3 Give children their decorated planters. Have them fill their planter just over half-full with play dough "soil." Then help them push the bare end of their paint stirrer into the soil so that it stands upright.

Book Links

Jack's Garden
by Henry Cole
(HarperCollins, 1997)
Using the rhyming pattern of "This Is the House That Jack Built," this garden book shows how the parts of nature connect and grow together.

I'm Growing!
by Aliki
(HarperCollins, 1992)
Our arms, legs, hair, toenails, muscles, bones, and skin all grow from the moment we are born. This book offers a simple explanation of how and why we grow.

How Kids Grow
by Jean Marzollo
(Cartwheel Books, 1998)
Photographs show how children grow and change from tiny babies to six- and seven-year-olds.

When I Was Little: A Four-Year-Old's Memoir of Her Youth
by Jamie Lee Curtis
(HarperCollins, 1993)
A young girl celebrates her sense of self by comparing what she can do now to the things she did "when she was little."

4 Provide each child with a set of mini clothespins equal to his or her age. Help children clip each age card to the corresponding number marker on the ruler.

Using the Project

Invite children to use the pictures on their planters to tell about things they've learned to do over the years. What were they able to do at age one, two, three, and so on? Afterward, display the planters in a special classroom "garden."

Who's That?
Chair-Back Covers
pages 7–8

Through the Years
Picture Mobiles
pages 9–11

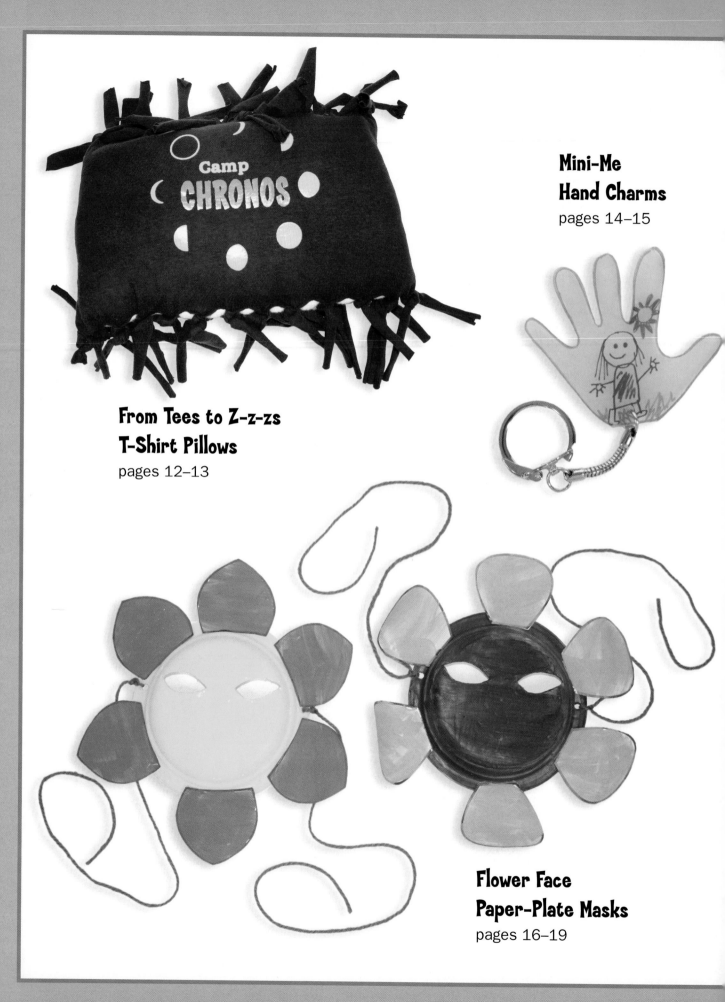

**Mini-Me
Hand Charms**
pages 14–15

**From Tees to Z-z-zs
T-Shirt Pillows**
pages 12–13

**Flower Face
Paper-Plate Masks**
pages 16–19

My Shadow
Silhouette Portraits

pages 20–22

Found-Letter
Nameplates

pages 23–24

My Thoughts and Dreams
Personalized Collages
pages 25–26

Watch Me Grow
Picture Planters
pages 30–33

Patchwork Me
Nine-Square Quilts
pages 27–29

My Favorite Things
Tissue-Box Frames
pages 34–35

Special People
Community Tree
pages 36–40

My Changing Moods
Paper-Plate Faces
pages 41–45

I Love My Locks!
Hair Model
pages 46–47

My Family
Finger Puppets
pages 48–50

Friends Forever!
Keepsake Book
pages 51–53

I like when we play
with blocks.
Tania

Stepping Out
Stationery
pages 54–56

Personalized Pal
Stand-Up Paper Models
pages 57–59

I Can Do It!
Moxie Magnets
pages 60–61

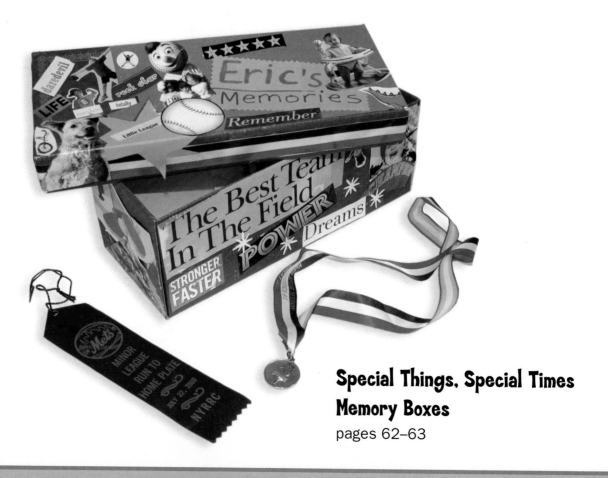

Special Things, Special Times
Memory Boxes
pages 62–63

Watch me grow!

6

5

4

3

2

1

Ruler and Leaves

My Favorite Things Tissue-Box Frames

Children transform a tissue box and their favorite trinkets into a personalized picture frame.

Materials

- one tissue-box cube per child
- small trinkets such as plastic toys, decorative buttons, costume jewelry, plastic blocks, stickers, and so on (brought from home by children)
- craft glue
- 4- by 6-inch photo of each child (brought from home)
- clear tape
- scissors

Tip

You might snap digital photos of children and make 4- by 6-inch color copies to use for this project.

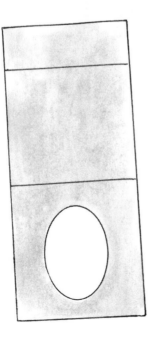

Before You Start

1 Take a picture of each child, or send a note home to families to request a 4- by 6-inch photo, explaining that it will be used in a project. Also, ask families to help their child gather a few small, lightweight items (such as buttons, costume jewelry, stickers, and so on) that they like and can bring to school to use in the project. You might request donations of empty tissue-box cubes, too.

2 Enlist adult volunteers to cut off the top, one side, and bottom of each tissue box so that the three sections make one long continuous strip. Then have them trim away all but 3 inches of the bottom section (see illustration, left). Ask them to also remove any plastic around the opening.

3 Gather a supply of extra trinkets to have on hand for use by children who forget or are unable to bring in their own.

4 Bring in one or two of your own favorite trinkets to share with children.

Introducing the Project

Tell children that most people have a few favorite things that have special meaning to them. Show them your own special trinkets, explaining why they are special to you. Then invite children to tell about one trinket that has meaning to them. If they brought it for the project, let them show it to the class at this time. After sharing, tell children that they'll make a special frame to showcase their picture as well as a few of their favorite things.

Making the Project

1 Work with children individually or in small groups. Cover each table with newspaper. Then give children a precut tissue-box strip and the trinkets they brought from home. Provide additional trinkets for children who need them.

2 To make a frame, have children glue their trinkets on only the section of the tissue-box with the opening. Encourage them to fill in the space surrounding the opening, but not to glue anything in the opening. Allow the glue to dry.

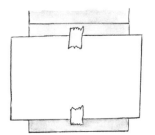

3 Give children their photos. Have them tape their photo behind the tissue-box opening to frame their picture. Then help them trim away the edges of their photo to fit the frame.

4 Ask children to fold the other two sections of the frame to form a pyramid, with the framed picture facing outward and the short bottom section serving as a base. Help children tape the bottom edge in place.

Using the Project

Ask children to share their frames with the class, telling about the things they used to decorate them. Encourage them to tell how each item is, or reminds them of, one of their favorite things. Later, invite children to take their frames home or to present them to family members as a gift.

Book Links

Snowballs
by Lois Ehlert
(Harcourt, 1999)
A whole snow family is created from found objects—like buttons, fabric, and seeds—and a little imagination.

School Picture Day
by Lynn Plourde
(Dutton, 2002)
Josephina's nonconformity is put to good use in this rambunctious read-aloud about school picture day.

Cool Scrapbooks
by Pam Price
(Checkerboard Books, 2004)
This book introduces readers to fun craft projects with step-by-step instructions and accompanying photographs.

Special People Community Tree

Children branch out to celebrate the community of people who help them grow.

- tree trunk, branch, limb, and leaf patterns (pages 38–40)
- 9- by 12- inch tagboard
- green construction paper
- photos of individual family members, friends, teachers, and so on (brought in by each child)
- 3- by 5-inch plain index cards
- color markers, colored pencils, and crayons
- glue sticks

Tips

- *Work with children in groups of four or fewer to make the project.*
- *For sturdier trees, use recyclable cardboard instead of tagboard to make the tree trunk and limbs.*

Before You Start

1 Ask children to bring in pictures of themselves, family members (siblings, parents, and grandparents), friends, and other special people in their lives. You can send a note to families to request the photos (or copies of photos), explaining that the images will be used in a project. Ask them to send pictures of individuals, rather than group pictures.

2 Copy the tree trunk, branch, and limb patterns (pages 38–39) onto tagboard and the leaf patterns (page 40) onto green construction paper. Then enlist volunteers to precut the trunks, branches, limbs, and leaves, cutting out one trunk, several branches and limbs of each size, and several leaves for each child. If your copy machine doesn't take tagboard or construction paper, make tagboard templates of the patterns. Then have volunteers trace and cut out the shapes.

Introducing the Project

Invite children to tell about some of the people who are important in their lives. Are these special people family members? Friends? Neighbors? Are they children or adults? Then tell children that the people close to their own age— their brothers, sisters, and classmate—belong to the same *generation*, a group of people who were born around the same time. Explain that their parents belong to another generation, and their grandparents to still another generation. Finally, tell children that they will create a "community" tree to celebrate the special people in their lives.

Making the Project

1 Divide the class into small groups. Give children their pictures and have them sort the people in their pictures into two groups: their own generation and the adult generation. If children did not bring pictures, invite them to use color markers, colored pencils, and crayons to draw pictures of a few individuals—themselves, siblings, classmates, parents, and so on—on 3- by 5-inch index cards.

2 Give each child a tree trunk cutout. Have children glue the pictures of people belonging to their generation (children) on the trunk. These pictures might include their brothers, sisters, and friends since they are in the same generation.

3 Ask children to glue each picture of a person from an older generation to a leaf and write that person's name on the leaf. These pictures might include parents, grandparents, teachers, and other adults.

4 Have children glue each leaf to the end of a small limb.

5 To assemble their tree, have children glue several branches to the trunk, extending them outward and upward (as shown). Then help them glue each limb (with its leaf and photo attached) to one of the branches.

Using the Project

Display the community trees around the room. Invite children to use their community tree to share about their family, friends, and other special people in their lives and to tell what generation each belongs to—their own or an older generation.

Book Links

The Ancestor Tree
by T. Obinkaram Echewa
(Penguin, 1994)
A contemporary folktale about how customs begin, change, and end, as well as what it means to be an ancestor.

The Grandad Tree
by Trish Cooke
(Candlewick, 2000)
A thoughtful explanation of how memories of special people can endure long after they are gone.

The Family Reunion
by Tricia Tusa
(Turtleback Books, 1993)
No one quite remembers some guests who show up at a large family's reunion. But after some crazy reminiscing, the guests realize they're in the wrong place!

Tree Trunk

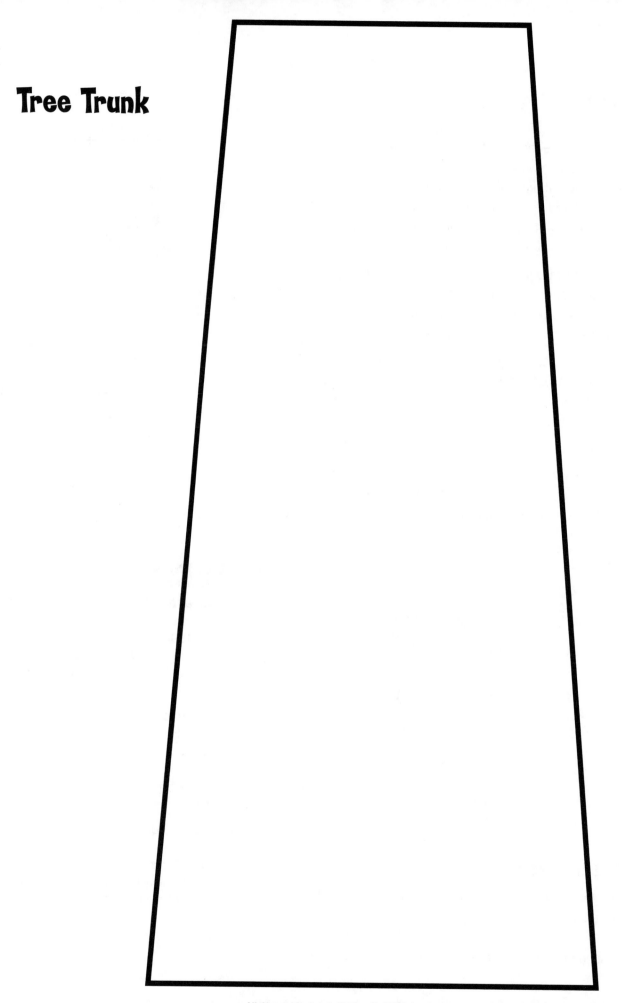

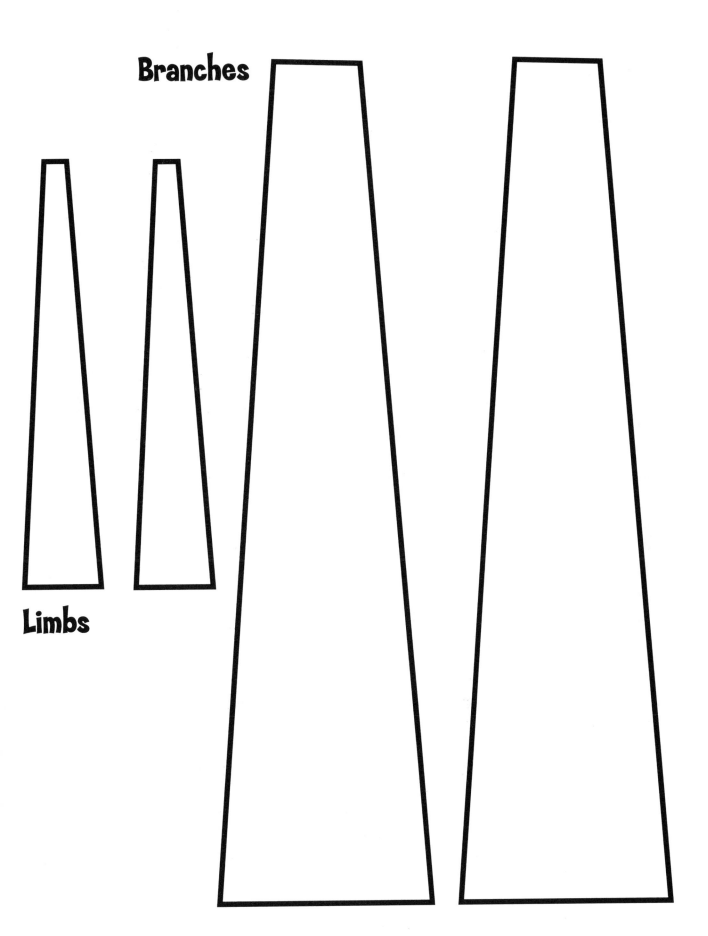

Branches

Limbs

Leaves

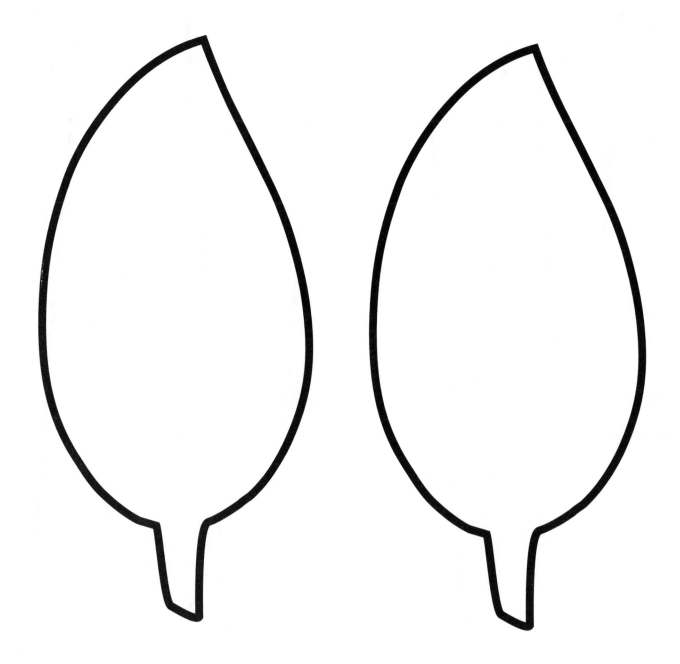

My Changing Moods Paper-Plate Faces

Kids explore how facial expressions can show different emotions.

Before You Start

1 Enlist volunteers to mark each paper plate for eye and nose placement. To do this, have them draw a cross on the inside of each plate to mark the center. Then ask them to use a blunt-point pencil to make a small indentation to show where each eye should be placed. Each indentation should be about an inch away from the center vertical line (one on the left and the other on the right) and just above the horizontal line. Finally, ask them to turn over the plate and draw a light line to show where children should draw a nose.

2 Copy a set of the eyebrow and mouth patterns for each child.

Introducing the Project

Pair up children to guide them in exploring how facial features help them express feelings. Ask the partners to sit facing each other and then make a happy face. Have them describe the features that show happiness on their partner's face. How do the eyebrows and mouth look? Next, have the partners make a sad face. Now what do they see? How are the eyebrows and mouth different from the happy face? Finally, ask the partners to make mad faces, describe what they see, and compare the features to their happy and sad facial expressions. Afterward, tell children that they will make paper-plate faces that can be used to show different emotions.

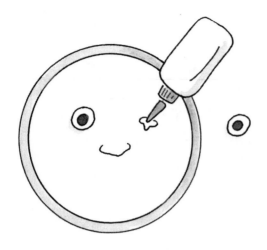

Making the Project

Day One

1 Give each child a paper plate and point out the indentations and marked area on it. Tell children they will decorate the plate to represent themselves. Have children use a dark color to draw their nose where the light line is marked. Then have them color the plate to resemble their skin color.

2 Help children use white glue to affix the wiggle eyes over the indentations on the plate.

3 Ask children to pick out a yarn color to match their own hair color. Have them cut the yarn in lengths to represent the length of their hair. When they are ready to glue the hair onto their paper-plate face, have children turn their plate over and glue the ends of the yarn to the top back rim. Allow the glue to dry.

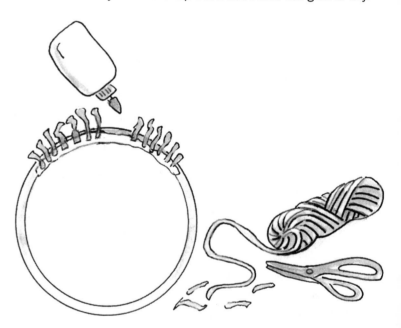

Book Links

Ed Emberley's Drawing Book of Faces
by Ed Emberley
(Little Brown & Co., 1975)
This book gives simple, step-by-step instructions for drawing a variety of faces that reflect different emotions.

Smiling
by Gwenyth Swain
(Carolrhoda Books, 1999)
Simple text and photos of children around the world feature reasons why people smile.

Funny Faces: A Very First Picture Book
by Nicola Tuxworth
(Gareth Stevens, 1999)
Photographs and simple text show how babies' faces can reveal their feelings and moods.

Day Two

1 Pass out the eyebrow and mouth strips. Ask children to color all the strips the same skin color that they used on their paper-plate face.

2 Have them use a crayon or marker color that matches their hair color to trace the eyebrow lines on the eyebrow strips. They should also trace the mouth lines with a color that matches their lip color.

3 Help children cut out all the strips, putting all the eyebrow strips in one stack and the mouth strips in another. Have them use a glue stick to glue each stack of strips together along the left edge only. Then help them glue the stack of eyebrows to the upper left side of their paper-plate faces and the stack of mouths to the lower left side, aligning the curve of the strips to the curve of the plate. The right edge of the strips should be loose so children can flip them back and forth.

4 Invite children to cut out ear shapes from 3- by 4-inch pieces of construction paper that match their skin color. If desired, they can add details to their ear cutouts. Then have children glue the ears to the sides of their paper-plate faces, being careful not to trap the eyebrow or mouth strips.

Using the Project

Invite children to flip and combine different eyebrow and mouth strips on their paper-plate faces to make various expressions. Ask them to describe the moods that the expressions might represent.

More Book Links

The Many Faces of the Face: Art for Children Series
by Brigitte Baumbusch
(Stewart, Tabori & Chang, 1999)
Art from around the globe—from ancient to contemporary times, and in a wide range of mediums—presents a variety of ways in which the face has been depicted.

Today I Feel Silly & And Other Moods That Make My Day
by Jamie Lee Curtis
(HarperCollins, 1998)
Readers view a range of changing emotions— from silly to anger to excitement—through a young girl's experiences. A mood wheel in the back allows readers to change the girl's expressions.

When Sophie Gets Angry—Really, Really Angry
by Molly Bang
(Scholastic, 2004)
When a young girl gets upset, she manages her anger by taking time to cool off and regain her composure.

Eyebrows

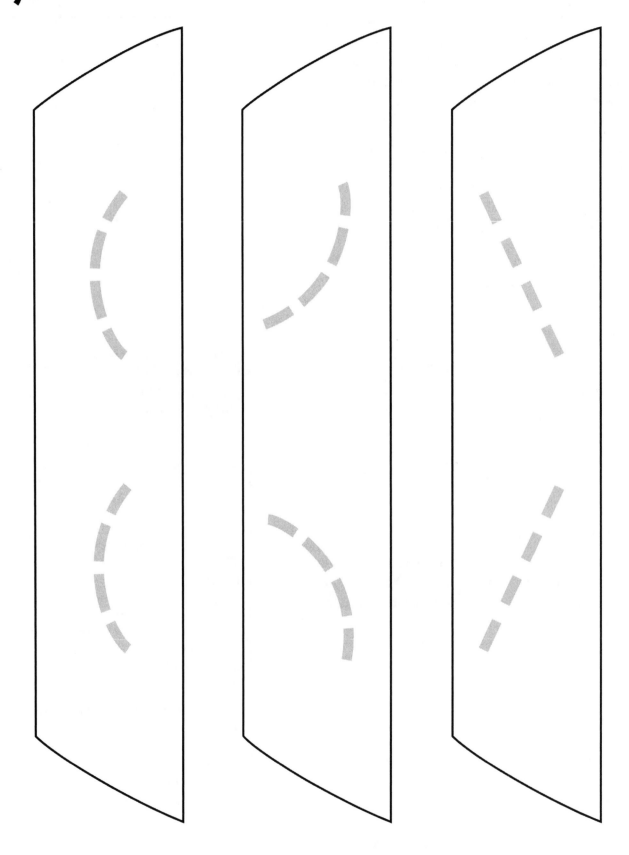

Mouths

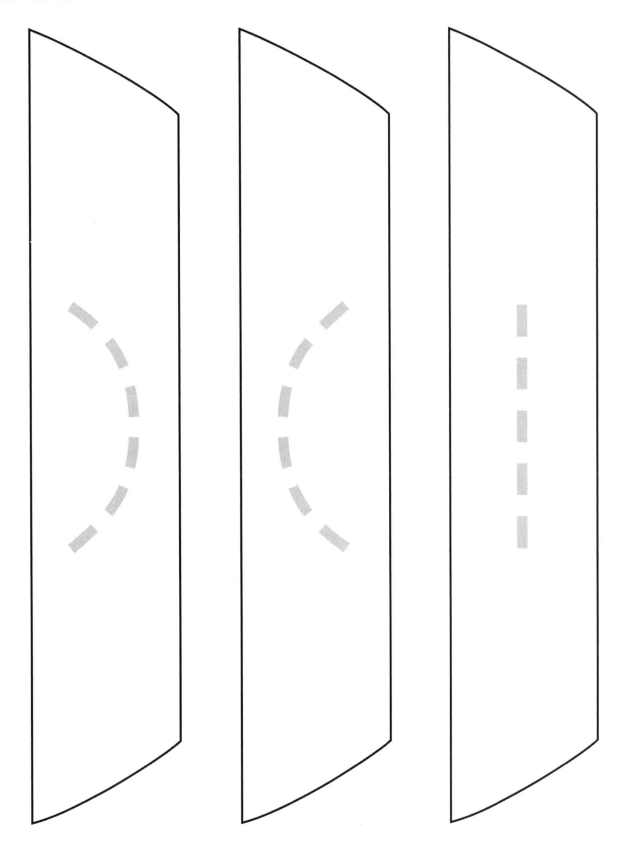

I Love My Locks! Hair Model

Whether children have long, short, straight, or curly hair, they can celebrate their different "dos" with this simple project.

Tip

Work with children in groups of four or fewer to do this project.

Before You Start

1 You might ask school workers and parents to donate yogurt containers for this project. While regular containers can be used, contoured containers, such as the Danimals® containers, work best.

2 Remove the labels from the yogurt containers.

Introducing the Project

To jumpstart a discussion about hair, share one or more of the books in Book Links (see page 47). Then invite children to describe their hair. (If desired, have children look at themselves in an unbreakable hand mirror as they do this.) What color is their hair? Is it long, short, or medium length? Is it straight or curly? Ask children to tell how their hair contributes to their own uniqueness. Wrap up the discussion by telling children that they will make a special model of themselves to showcase their hair.

Making the Project

1 Divide the class into small groups. Give each child a yogurt container and two wiggle eyes. Instruct children to use glue dots to affix the wiggle eyes to the container, as shown.

2 Have children use a permanent marker to add a mouth, nose, and eyebrows to create a face on their container. They might also color the bottom of the container to resemble a shirt.

3 Provide groups with pencils, rulers, scissors, tape, and the different sizes of yellow, orange, tan, brown, and black construction paper. Ask children to select a strip of construction paper that most closely matches their own hair color and length. Children with long hair should choose a wide strip and those with short hair should select a narrow strip of paper.

4 Help children use the ruler and pencil to draw a line about an inch away from one long edge of their paper strip.

5 Have children fringe their strip of paper to create hair, starting their cuts at the unmarked edge of the paper and stopping at the penciled line on the opposite side. Have them fringe-cut along the entire length of the paper.

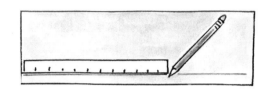

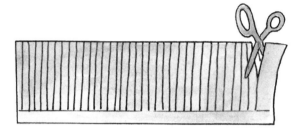

6 Show children how to roll their fringed paper, as shown. Have them fit the uncut end into the top of their yogurt container and release the roll so that it expands to fit snugly into the opening. Help them remove the roll of paper hair, holding it to prevent the roll from expanding more. Have them tape the outer edge to secure the roll and then reinsert the "hair" into the container.

7 Invite children to work with the hair to make it better match their hair length or texture. They might wrap the paper strands around a pencil to make curls, or trim the hair for a better length match.

Using the Project

Invite children to use their projects to describe their hair color, length, and texture. Then create a three-column chart titled "Hair" with the headings "Short," "Medium," and "Long." Have children write their name in the column that best describes the length of their hair. Afterward, compare the results to see which length of hair is the most common in your class. Later, you might work with children to chart hair color or hair texture (straight or curly).

Book Links

Hairs/Pelitos
by Sandra Cisneros
(Random House, 1997)
This bilingual story describes the differences between family members' hair, teaching children that diversity can extend from family to community and beyond.

Crazy Hair Day
by Barney Saltzberg
(Candlewick Press, 2003)
Stanley fixes his hair in a colorful, wacky style for Crazy Hair Day at school. But he realizes—too late—that he wore his special "do" on the wrong day!

I Love My Hair
by Natasha Anastasia Tarpley
(Little Brown, 1998)
A mother teaches her troubled daughter to love her hair and celebrate her African-American heritage.

Nappy Hair
by Carolivia Herron
(Dragonfly Books, 1998)
Told in a call-and-response dialogue, this empowering story tells about how a girl's nappy hair came to be.

My Family Finger Puppets

Kids can introduce others to their families and act out fun stories with these easy-to-make finger puppets.

Materials

- puppet patterns (page 50)
- one sheet of tagboard per child
- color markers and crayons
- scissors
- clear tape

Tips

- *Work with children in groups of four or fewer to make the project.*
- *Before taping the ends of the finger puppets together, you might laminate them for durability.*

Before You Start

1 Copy a set of puppet patterns on tagboard for each child. If your copy machine doesn't take tagboard, copy the patterns on white copy paper. Children can decorate their puppets, glue them to tagboard, and then cut them out.

2 You might arrange to have adult volunteers come in to help children cut out and assemble their finger puppets.

Introducing the Project

Ask children to define *family* and to tell what kind of people make up a family. Help them understand that families might consist of people who are related, such as parents, siblings, grandparents, cousins, as well as those who might not be related, such as close friends, caregivers, and so on. In addition, some families even include pets! After discussing, share Todd Parr's *The Family Book* or any other book of your choice about families (see Book Links, page 49). Then invite children to create a finger puppet family to represent their own family.

Making the Project

1 Divide the class into small groups. Give each child a set of finger-puppet patterns. Point out that the patterns represent people and pets, and that the people patterns come in different sizes. Invite children to tell why they think the people puppets vary in size. Then ask children to name five or fewer members in their family that they'd like to make finger puppet models of. (Remind them that families might consist of related or unrelated members.) Help them decide which pattern they might use for each family member. If needed, provide additional copies to give children more options.

2 Invite children to use color markers or crayons to create a finger puppet for each family member of their choice. Encourage them to include details that represent that family member, such as facial features, hair, clothing, and so on.

3 Help children carefully cut out each of their finger puppets. Have them work with partners to fit the bottom of each puppet around one of their fingers and tape the ends in place. If needed, they can trim the ends to create a snugger fit.

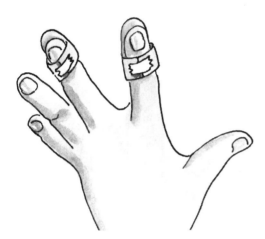

Using the Project

Invite children to introduce one family member at a time to the class by putting that puppet on their finger and telling something about him or her. Afterward, children might use their finger-puppet family to act out scenes from home (such as mealtimes or family activities) or invent stories to act out. Encourage children to perform their finger-puppet acts for small groups.

Book Links

And Tango Makes Three
by Justin Richardson
(Simon & Schuster, 2005)
A true story about two male penguins that adopt an unwanted baby penguin. This is a story from which many can learn tolerance.

Families
by Ann Morris
(HarperCollins, 2000)
This look at families from all over the world offers a glimpse into the rich variety of cultures and helps children consider their own families.

The Family Book
by Todd Parr
(Little, Brown & Company, 2003)
This concept book celebrates the diversity of family groups in a fun, silly, and reassuring way.

You're Not My Real Mother!
by Molly Friedrich
(Little, Brown & Co, 2004)
This conversation offers a response to children who've ever asked why they don't look like their adoptive parents and helps readers explore the emotional realities of a different kind of family.

Finger Puppets

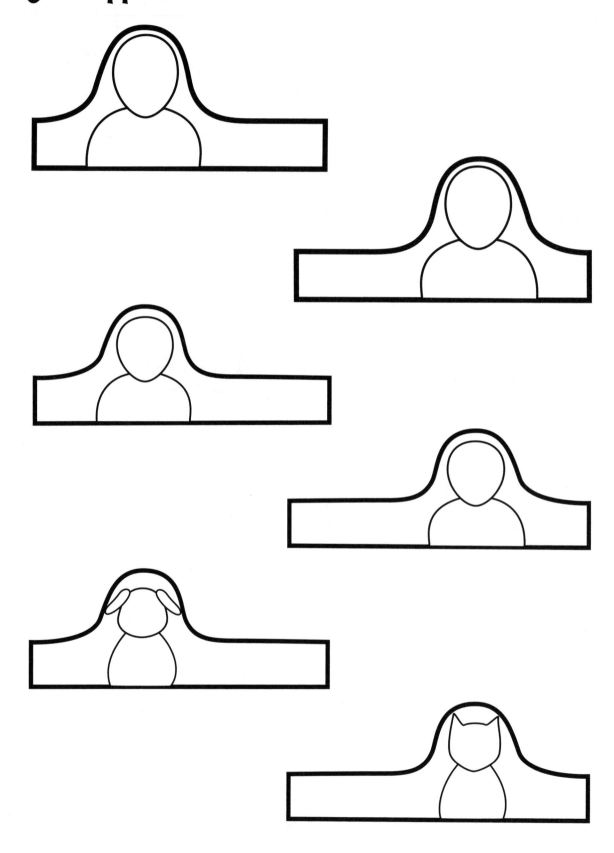

Friends Forever! Keepsake Book

Children express their friendship with classmates in these unique, personalized books.

Before You Start

1 Enlist volunteers to use a hole punch to make holes in the 9- by 12-inch sheets of construction paper, cardboard, and decorative paper. Have them punch two holes along one short edge of the sheets, aligning the pages so that the holes are in the same place on all pages (see illustration on page 53).

2 You might arrange to have volunteers come in to help children assemble their books.

Introducing the Project

Discuss friendship with children. What does it mean to be a friend? What are the characteristics of a friend? Can they give examples of actions or words that exhibit friendship? Work with children to create a list of qualities that help define a friend. Then invite them to tell about ways they show friendship or have been shown friendship by others. Finally, tell children that they will work together to help each other create a book to celebrate friendship.

Making the Project

Day One

1 Divide the class into groups of six. Cover each table with newspaper. For each group, cover the bottom of a few plates with paint and place the plates on their table. Ask children to choose six sheets of construction paper in the colors of their choice.

2 Have children place one sheet of paper at a time in front of them, with the holes on their left side. Invite them to make a paint handprint on the paper using the paint color of their choice. Encourage them to spread their fingers and press their hand firmly, placing it just to the right of the holes, to create a well-defined handprint.

Materials

Day One
- six sheets of 9- by 12-inch construction per child (light colors work best)
- tempera paint in assorted colors
- foam or plastic plates, one per paint color for each group

Day Two
- one 9- by 12-inch sheet of cardboard per child
- one 9- by 12-inch sheet of decorative paper per child
- color markers
- one wide craft stick per child
- one wide rubber band per child

Tip

String up a clothesline to hang children's handprints on to dry.

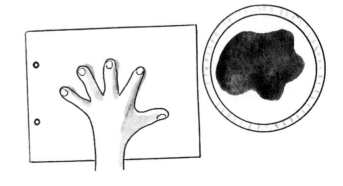

3 Repeat to make a handprint on each of the six sheets of construction paper. Help children write their name in pencil on a back corner of each page.

4 Set the handprints aside to dry.

Day Two

1 Assemble children back into their groups. Give them their six pages of handprints. Then invite one child at a time to distribute his or her pages to the other members of the group, and also pass one page to you.

2 Ask each group member to write (or dictate) a message of friendship on the child's page. They might write about a special way they share friendship with the child. Or have group members draw a picture to show friendship. Before children begin to work, check that they have the pages upright (with holes on left). Remind them to sign their name to their message and then return the completed page to the child. When finished, each child should have a special message on each of his or her six handprint pages.

Book Links

Frog and Toad Are Friends
by Arnold Lobel
(HarperTrophy, 1979)
These five warm, humorous stories highlight the friendship between Frog and Toad.

George and Martha
by James Marshall
(Houghton Mifflin, 1974)
Two lovable hippos teach the meaning of friendship in five separate stories.

What's the Recipe for Friends?
by Greg M. Williamson
(Peerless Publishing, 1999)
The new kid in school follows his mom's recipe for making friends, and by the end of the first week, the young boy has a new friend!

I Like You
by Sandol Stoddard
Houghton Mifflin, 1990
This little book is full of delightful ways to show and share friendship.

3 Pass out a sheet of cardboard and decorative paper to each child. Help children write a title, such as "My Friends at School," and their name on the decorative paper to create a book cover.

4 To assemble the book, help children stack their handprint pages between their cover and the cardboard, which will serve as a back cover. Check that the all the holes line up along the left edge of the stack.

5 Give children a craft stick and rubber band. Show them how to loop the rubber band over one end of the craft stick. Then, working from the front of the unbound book, have children thread the loose end of the rubber band through the top hole in the stack and then back up through the bottom hole. Finally, help children stretch and loop the loose end of the rubber band over the other end of the craft stick.

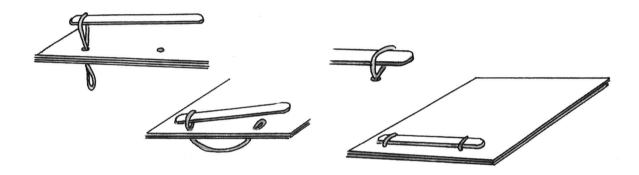

Expanding the Project

If desired, have children include a page from every classmate in their book. To do this, rearrange the groups so that children are working with different classmates. Have them repeat all the steps through Day Two, step 2. Then help them carefully take apart their books, add the new pages between the covers, and reassemble it.

Using the Project

Invite group members to read their friendship books with each other and then talk about their friendship experiences. Later, they can share their books with other members of the class.

Stepping Out Stationery

Oh, the places kids can go with these textured, shoe-shaped notes designed to travel near and far.

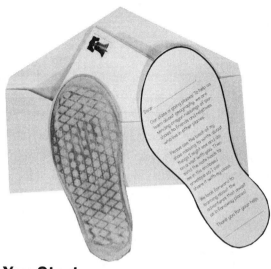

Before You Start

1 Send a note home to families to request that they send two stamped, addressed envelopes to school. Ask them to address one envelope to their child and the other to a relative or friend selected by their child. Explain that the relative or friend should live in a different city or state.

2 Copy and cut out the "Stepping Out" note on page 56 for each child.

3 Bring in extra envelopes and stamps for children who forget or are unable to bring in their own. You might also have a list of pen pals from other places handy for children to use.

4 If desired, bring in a few new or little-worn shoes that have textured soles. Invite children to use these shoes—instead of their own—to make their crayon rubbings.

Introducing the Project

Display a map of the United States or a world map. Or show children a globe. Help them find the city (or state) in which their school is located. Encourage children to share about other cities, states, or countries they might have lived in or visited. Help them locate some of these places on the map or globe. Then ask if they have relatives or friends in other places. As children respond, ask where the person lives and work with children to locate that place. Invite them to tell about visits they may have made to these locations and what kind of things they did there. Afterward, tell children that they will create special notes to send family or friends who live in other places.

Making the Project

1 Divide the class into small groups. Provide each group with construction paper, peeled crayons, and scissors. Then ask children to remove one shoe. Help them trace the outline of their shoe on a sheet of construction paper.

2 Have children turn their shoe upside down and examine the design on its sole. Then show them how to make a crayon rubbing of the design by placing the outline of their shoe on top of the sole of their shoe and then firmly rubbing the side of a crayon over the paper. As children work, the textured pattern from their shoe will appear on the paper.

3 Have children cut out their shoe outline and write their name along one edge of the decorated side.

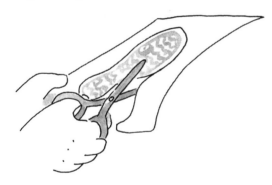

4 Work with each child to fill in a copy of the note. Help children fold their note, shoe cutout, and self-addressed envelope. Have them insert these items in the other envelope.

Using the Project

Plan a class trip to a local post office or drop box to mail the letters. Remind children to bring in their returned "Stepping Out" notes (and envelopes) to share with the class. Before reading each enclosed note, check the envelope to learn from where it was sent. Then help children find that location on a map or globe. Finally, read the note aloud and discuss its contents.

Book Links

Flat Stanley
by Jeff Brown
(Scholastic, 1974)
After being flattened by a bulletin board, Flat Stanley discovers he can enjoy new adventures doing things that others are unable to do.

Mailing May
by Michael O. Tunnell
(HarperTrophy, 2000)
May's family can't afford a train ticket, so they mail the young girl to her grandmother's house! This is based on a true story in 1914.

There's a Map on My Lap!: All About Maps
by Tish Rabe
(Random House, 2002)
The Cat in the Hat introduces beginning readers to different kind of maps in fun and memorable ways.

"Stepping Out" Note

Dear _____ ,

Our class is going places! To help us learn about geography, we are sending crayon rubbings of our shoes to friends and relatives who live in other places.

Please use the back of my shoe rubbing to write about things I might see and do on a visit with you. Then send the note back to me in the enclosed envelope so I can share it with my class.

We look forward to learning about the adventures that await us in faraway places!

Thank you for your help,

_____

Personalized Pal Stand-Up Paper Models

Children can use these unique paper models of themselves to role-play their favorite activities.

Before You Start

1 Ask children to bring in a picture of themselves. You can send a note to families to request the photo (or a copy of a photo), explaining that the size of the child's head in the image should measure about 1 ½ inches wide. Tell them that the image will be cut and altered for the project.

2 Make one tagboard copy of the model and stand patterns (page 59) for each child. Then enlist volunteers to precut the patterns along the bold lines. Have them also cut along the broken line on both the model and stand cutouts. If your copy machine doesn't take tagboard, make tagboard templates of the patterns. Then have volunteers trace and cut out the shapes.

Introducing the Project

Ask children to tell about some of the things that make them unique. As they respond, steer them to consider the clothes they wear. Do they like to wear certain styles or colors that help them express their individuality? Invite children to describe ways that they exhibit their uniqueness through what they wear, either at school or when they are away from school. Wrap up the discussion by telling children that they will make stand-up paper models to represent themselves.

Making the Project

1 Divide the class into small groups and give children their photo. Help children cut around the hair and outline of their face in their photo to isolate their head from the rest of the picture.

Tips

- *Work with children in groups of four or fewer to make the project.*
- *If desired, invite children to create additional paper models to represent family members, friends, teachers, and so on.*

2 Give children a tagboard model. Tell them they will decorate the figure to represent themselves. Then have them glue their head cutout onto the head of the model.

3 Invite children to use color markers, colored pencils, crayons, and oil pastels to draw clothes onto their tagboard model. Encourage them to use colors and designs to create clothes that express their uniqueness. Also, have them use a flesh tone that matches their skin color to fill in areas like the neck or arms on their figure.

4 Show children how to fit the slits in the tagboard stand and their model together to make their figure freestanding.

Using the Project

Model different ways people might introduce themselves. Then invite them to use their personalized paper models to introduce themselves to the class. After their introduction, encourage children to tell about the clothes on their paper models, explaining how the colors, styles, and designs reflect their individuality. Later, small groups can use their models to role-play greetings and other activities. You might also have children pose their figures together to take a group snapshot of your paper-model class!

Book Links

The Spiffiest Giant in Town
by Julia Donaldson
(Dial Books for Young Readers, 2003)
On his way to buy new clothes, a big-hearted giant named George encounters various animals that need his help—and his clothes.

The Hundred Dresses
by Eleanor Estes
(Voyager Books, 1988)
In this book about kindness and standing up for what is right, a poor girl claims to have a hundred dresses at home when she's teased about wearing the same faded blue dress every day.

All Kinds of Clothes
by Jeri S. Cipriano
(Pebble Books, 2003)
Colorful photos and simple text relate history to the everyday world in this book that features clothing from around the world.

Model and Stand

I Can Do It! Moxie Magnets

These irresistible "stick-to-it" kids make fun refrigerator magnet gifts!

Materials

- photo of each child in the process of learning a skill or performing a recently learned skill (brought from home)
- one 4- by 6-inch piece of tagboard per child
- glue sticks
- scissors
- one 1-inch strip of magnetic tape per child

Tip

You might snap digital photos of children practicing or performing recently learned skills at school and print 4- by 6-inch color copies to use for this project.

Before You Start

Ask children to bring in a picture that shows them learning how to do something new or performing a newly learned skill or activity. Tell them that full-body shots work well for this project. You can send a note to families to request the photo (or copy of a photo), explaining that the image will be cut and altered for the project.

Introducing the Project

Discuss with children what *determination* means. Ask them to share some of their own experiences in which they showed determination—such as in learning to tie their shoe, write their name, pump their legs to swing, or ride a bike. Invite them to tell about difficulties or obstacles they might have had to overcome to achieve their goal. How long did they have to keep trying or practicing to learn the skill? If desired, read aloud *Mike Mulligan and His Steam Shovel* by Virginia Lee Burton (see Book Links, page 61) to share an example of how determination can help a person achieve something great. Then tell children that they will make special magnets to showcase their own "stick-to-it-iveness."

Making the Project

1 Give children their photo and a 4- by 6-inch piece of tagboard. Have them coat the back of their photo thoroughly with glue and then stick it to the tagboard. Allow the glue to dry.

2 Show children how to cut a loose outline around their image in the picture, cutting completely through the tagboard. Remind them to only cut away the background of the photo, leaving the image of themselves doing the pictured activity in one piece. When finished, children will have an interesting outline around their picture.

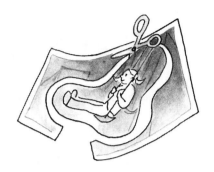

3 Give children a strip of magnetic tape. Have them peel the backing off the strip and then stick the magnet to the center back of their photo.

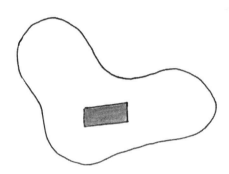

Using the Project

Invite children to show their magnets to the class. Encourage them to describe what they are doing in the photo and to tell about their experience in learning the skill or activity. Did they have to practice a lot? Did they ever get discouraged? How did they show determination in achieving their goal? Later, have children take their magnet home to share with their family and display on the refrigerator or other magnetic surface.

Book Links

The Little Engine That Could
by Watty Piper
(Grosset & Dunlap, 1978)
The Little Blue Engine overcomes odds when it pulls the train to the other side of the mountain saying, "I think I can–I think I can."

Mike Mulligan and His Steam Shovel
by Virginia Lee Burton
(Houghton Mifflin, 1939)
Mike Mulligan and his steam shovel team up to show a small town how old-fashioned hard work and ingenuity can measure up against progress.

Sink or Swim
by Valerie Coulman
(Lobster Press, 2005)
Although everyone tells Ralph that cows can't swim, he perseveres until he proves that cows can swim.

What Makes a Magnet?
by Franklyn M. Branley
(HarperTrophy, 1996)
Readers discover for themselves what makes a magnet. Hands-on activities include making a magnet and compass.

Special Things, Special Times Memory Boxes

These customized memory boxes are great for storing special keepsakes and mementos.

Tips

- *Work with children in groups of four or fewer to make the project.*
- *Each week, invite children to bring in a new item to share with the class and add to their memory box.*

Before You Start

1 Ask children to bring in a shoebox and its lid along with photos that represent special memories for them. (These might include people, pets, places, and so on.) You can send a note to families to request the photos (or copies of photos), explaining that the images may be cut or altered to make the project. Also ask them to send in a shoebox with a lid.

2 Bring in a few extra lidded shoeboxes to have on hand for children who forget or are unable to bring in their own.

3 On the day before doing the project, ask children to bring in a picture or small item that represents a special memory to them. Ask them to put the item in a paper lunch bag and write their name on the bag.

Introducing the Project

Ask children to take a few minutes to think about some of their favorite memories of people, pets, places, or experiences. Do they have pictures or special items that remind them of these things? Invite children to tell about a special object that represents a cherished memory for them. If desired, share about a special memory item of your own, as well. Then tell children that they will create personalized boxes in which they can store items that hold special memories for them.

Making the Project

1 Divide the class into small groups. Give children the shoebox and photos they brought in. Then provide each group with stickers, magazines, scissors, glue sticks, and color markers.

2 Invite children to remove the lid from their box. Have them decorate the outside of their box and lid with images, drawings, and designs that help depict who they are, what they are like, their experiences, their favorite activities, colors, food, and so on. They can glue on photos—or cut-out sections of their photos, as well as pictures cut or torn out of magazines, their own drawings and artwork, stickers, or words that describe them in some way.

3 Help children use markers and a strip of drawing paper to make a label for their box that says "_____'s Memories," using their own name on the label. Have them glue the label to their shoebox lid.

4 Give children the paper bag that holds their special memory item. Ask them to remove the item, place it in their memory box, and then put the lid on the box.

Using the Project

During sharing time, invite children to show their memory box to the class. Encourage them to tell how the images on the box represent them. Then ask them to open the box, remove the memory item inside, and share about the memory the item holds for them. When finished, have children return their item to the box and close the lid. You might have children replace the item in their box each week, or add a new item.

Book Links

The Memory String
by Eve Bunting
(Houghton Mifflin, 2000)
Laura learns that a "memory string" of buttons not only represents her past family history, but is also a way to record new memories.

When I Am Old With You
by Angela Johnson
(Scholastic, 1993)
A young boy and his grandfather look at old family photographs and clothes passed down from father to father. The story illustrates how traditions pass from one generation to the next and help shape individual identity.

Notes